D0349072

WHO WERE THE

ANCIENT GREEKS?

First published in 2006
in the UK by Franklin Watts
338 Euston Road, London NW1 3BH

Franklin Watts Australia, Hachette Children's Books
Level 17/207 Kent Street, Sydney NSW 2000

This series was devised and produced by McRae Books Srl,
Borgo S. Croce, 8, Florence (Italy)
Publishers: Anne McRae and Marco Nardi
Text: Loredana Agosta and Anne McRae
Main Illustrations: Lorenzo Cecchi, Matteo Chesi,
Ferruccio Cucchiarini, Inklink, MM comunicazione
(Manuela Cappon, Monica Favilli), Francesca D'Ottavi,
Paola Ravaglia
Illustrations: Studio Stalio (Alessandro Cantucci,
Fabiano Fabbrucci, Margherita Salvadori)

Design: Marco Nardi. Layout: Rebecca Milner
Colour separations: Fotolito Toscana, Firenze

A CIP catalogue record for this book is available
from the British Library.
Dewey Decimal Classification Number: 938

ISBN 0 7496 6788 5
ISBN-13 978 0 7496 6788 7

Printed and bound in Italy.

WHO WERE THE
ANCIENT GREEKS?

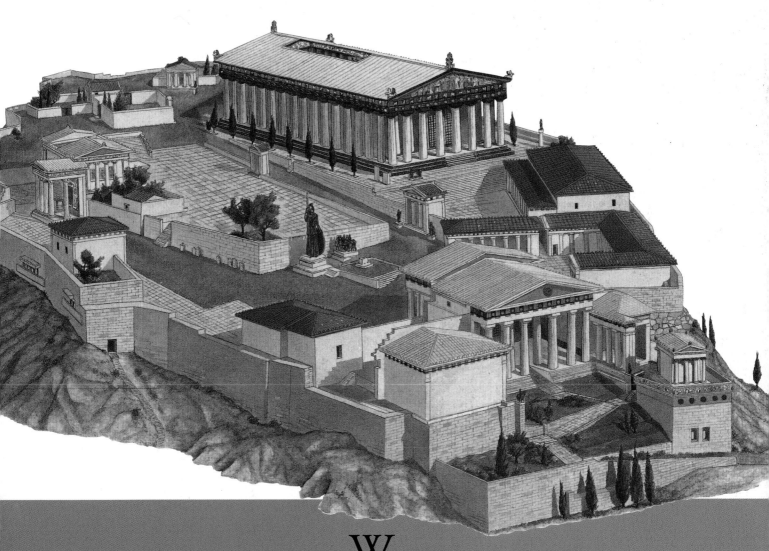

W
FRANKLIN WATTS
LONDON • SYDNEY

Archaic Greece
see pages 10-11

Knowledge
see page 24

The Ancient Greek World

- Greek homeland
- Greek colonies

BLACK SEA

• Troy

MAGNA GRAECIA

Delphi • Thebes
Corinth • • Athens
Olympia • • Argos
• Syracuse
Sparta   CYCLADES
ISLANDS
RHODES
CRETE

MEDITERRANEAN SEA

NORTH AFRICA

World Map

Greek Colonies
see page 13

Warriors and War see pages 20-21

Greek Colonies see page 13

Contents

Art and Architecture see page 19

Food and Farming see page 27

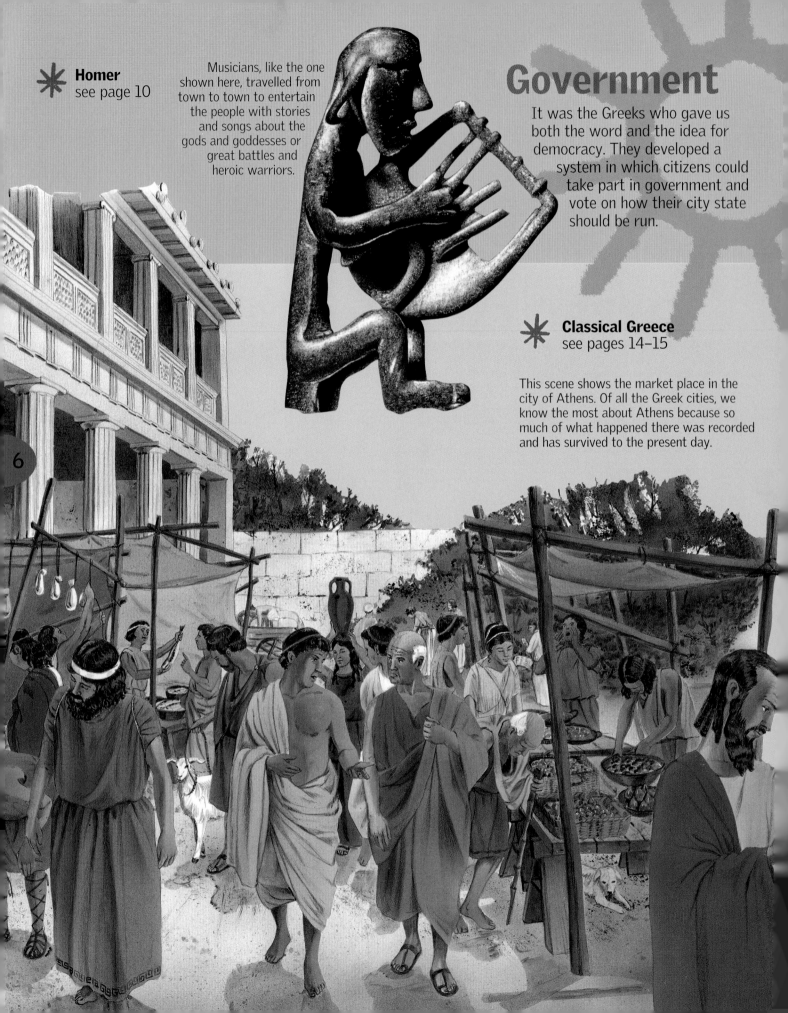

✳ **Homer**
see page 10

Musicians, like the one shown here, travelled from town to town to entertain the people with stories and songs about the gods and goddesses or great battles and heroic warriors.

Government

It was the Greeks who gave us both the word and the idea for democracy. They developed a system in which citizens could take part in government and vote on how their city state should be run.

✳ **Classical Greece**
see pages 14–15

This scene shows the market place in the city of Athens. Of all the Greek cities, we know the most about Athens because so much of what happened there was recorded and has survived to the present day.

Knowledge

Many aspects of modern life have their roots in ancient Greek learning and culture. The Greeks practically invented many fields of study, such as history and philosophy, and introduced many forms of literature, such as poetry and drama.

Science

Greek scientists first came up with many ideas that have since been proved correct. They were disciplined thinkers and wanted all their ideas to be confirmed by proof – just like modern scientists.

Gods and Goddesses
see page 16

The ancient Greeks worshipped many gods and goddesses. Each one was believed to help people with different aspects of daily life. The beautiful Artemis, below, protected women during childbirth.

Who were the ancient Greeks?

The ancient Greeks lived about 2,500 years ago in the Mediterranean lands of modern Greece and Turkey. Their splendid civilization developed in dozens of self-governing cities around the region, each having its own government, culture and distinct identity. Many of their ideas about government, knowledge, science and art led the way for many future generations.

7

Art

The ancient Greeks built magnificent temples, some of which are still standing. They also made statues and painted vases that tell stories about their gods and goddesses, or about daily life.

The vase painting on the left shows men in Athens voting. Not everyone was allowed to vote in ancient Athens; women and slaves were excluded.

Democracy
see page 15

The Cyclades Islands

One of the earliest civilizations developed on the Cyclades Islands. The people of the Cyclades had a rich culture but they left no written records, so we know very little about them. Many beautiful statues have survived from that time, mainly showing women and musicians.

Head carved by people of the Cyclades Islands.

This ornate drinking cup was found at a palace on the island of Crete.

The Mycenaeans

The war-like Mycenaean people conquered the Minoans on Crete in about 1450 BC. Their civilization consisted of a number of small kingdoms, each centred on a citadel, or fortified hilltop town. The great poet Homer (see page 10) told the story of how the mighty Mycenaean soldiers won a great victory against the Trojans during the Trojan War.

The Mycenaean soldiers built a huge wooden horse, hid inside it, and left it so that their enemies would find it and bring it inside their city. During the night, the Mycenaeans crept out and attacked the city of Troy.

The Minoans

The Minoans, named after the legendary King Minos, lived on the island of Crete. Their civilization was made up of many small states centred around palaces and ruled by kings. The palaces were surrounded by villages and farms. The Minoans were superb craftspeople and sailors, and traded far and wide.

Both the Minoans and the Mycenaeans used writing. The Minoan script, which archaeologists call Linear A (tablet, left, and disc, below), has never been understood. Mycenaean script, called Linear B, can be read and is an early form of Greek.

Before
the Greeks

Greek civilization did not just suddenly appear. Other civilizations had flourished in the region for thousands of years. The two main early Greek civilizations were those of the Minoans and the Mycenaeans. The Minoans lived on the island of Crete, while the Mycenaeans occupied both Crete and mainland Greece. Both were very advanced, with organized governments and armies, writing systems and trade links.

Timeline

Although real-life history does not divide itself neatly into exact periods, it can be useful to look at some general dates. This timeline shows the main civilizations and periods in ancient Greek history.

1) Cycladic civilization (3000–2000 BC)
2) Minoan civilization (2300–1450 BC)
3) Mycenaean civilization (1650–1200 BC)
4) The Greek "Dark Age" (1200–900 BC)
5) The Archaic period (900–480 BC)
6) The Classical period (480–334 BC)
7) The Hellenistic period (334–30 BC)

9

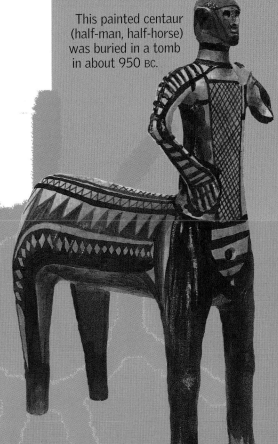

This painted centaur (half-man, half-horse) was buried in a tomb in about 950 BC.

The Dark Age

Mycenaean Greece ended abruptly in about 1200 BC. The next three hundred years are known as the "Dark Age". Little is known about the downfall of the Mycenaeans and the time after the collapse of their civilization. It was probably a period of unrest and migration. Even so, recent studies show that some rich and well-organized cities, such as the port city of Lefkandi, existed even then.

The best early potters and painters came from Athens. This vase shows the twin gods, Castor and Pollux, on horseback.

Pottery

Before the Archaic period, pottery was mainly decorated with geometric designs and patterns. Then painters began decorating vases with human figures, animals and scenes from Homer's poems. Artists decorated cups, olive-oil jars, water jars and bowls used for mixing wine and water.

Sculpture

Greek sculptors began carving stone and marble to create life-size statues of the gods and noble people. Archaic sculptors carved elegant and graceful figures. The smiling expression on some figures, known as the "Archaic smile", gives the figures a charming appearance.

Homer

The most famous Greek poet is Homer. He lived during the 8th or 9th century BC and composed the *Iliad* and the *Odyssey*. These two famous long poems about Greek gods and heroes became an important part of Greek culture and identity. They were retold by travelling entertainers and passed down to each generation by word of mouth. They were written down officially many years later.

According to tradition, Homer was blind. Some believe that he may have been a travelling entertainer himself.

Greek sculpture was painted. This sculpture of a woman, dating from Archaic times, still has some traces of paint.

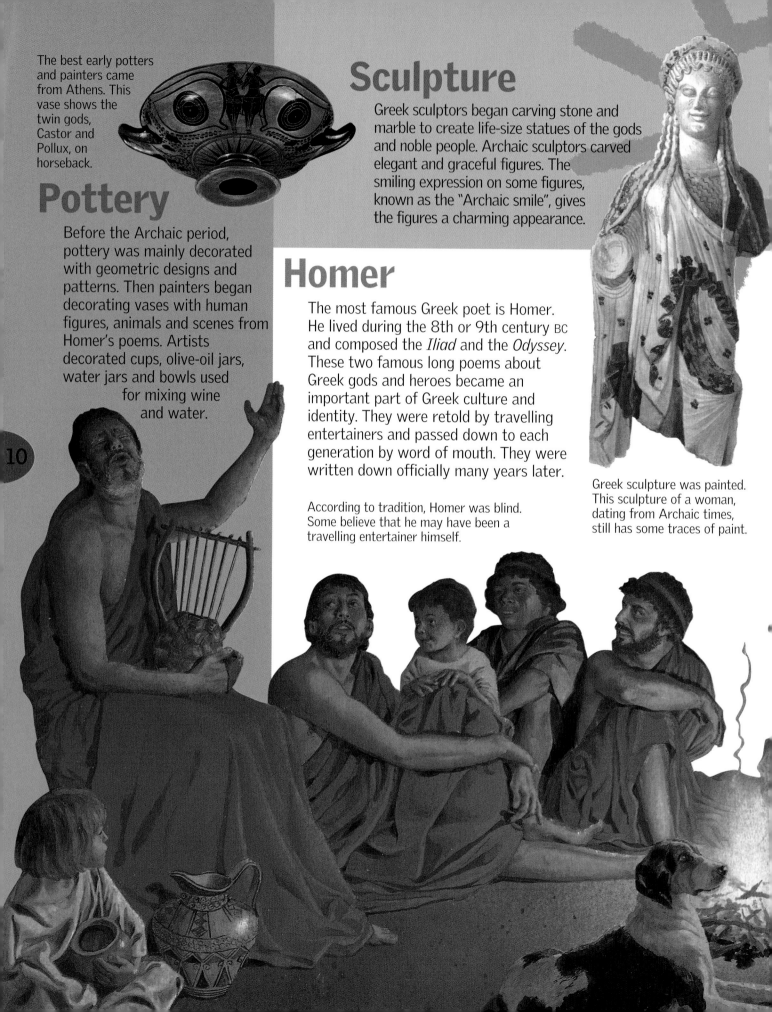

Olympic Games

During the Archaic period many city states held sporting events as part of religious festivals. The most famous games were the Olympic Games, held at Olympia in honour of the gods Zeus and Hera (see page 16). The festivities also included banquets and award ceremonies for the winners.

This is a detail of a vase which was given as a prize at the Olympic Games. It shows athletes competing in a horse race.

Archaic Times

By the end of the Dark Age people had begun to move from small, unprotected villages to fortified palaces. These settlements later developed into city states, or small nations, made up of an independent town and its surrounding countryside. During this time, known as the Archaic period, there were many cultural developments, especially in art and literature. Some of the major city states were Athens, Sparta, Corinth, Thebes and Argos.

City states

City states were surrounded by protective walls. Inside the walls there was a market place called the agora and an acropolis, or a hilltop site, where temples were constructed. Each city state had its own government and money. The first coins were made during the Archaic period. They were made of gold and silver and were used to buy things in the agora and for trade with other city states.

11

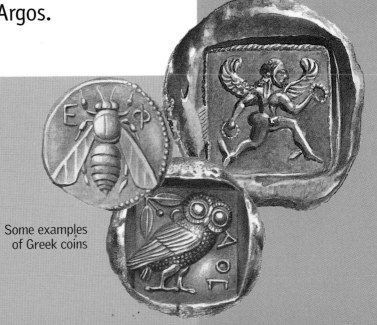

Some examples of Greek coins

Benefits

Farming in many areas of mainland Greece was difficult and wheat fields were too small to satisfy the growing population. Many colonies had good farmland so food from the colonies was sent to the mainland. Some colonies were also rich in natural resources, like metal and timber.

Settlers who migrated to the island of Sicily built magnificent temples like this one, dedicated to the Greek gods.

A Good Start

When a city state decided to set up a new colony, a basic plan was followed. First a group of people were selected to migrate to the new colony. Then a leader was chosen to arrange the voyage. He was assisted by officials who distributed the land and by priests who organized religious worship and rituals. Before the voyage, however, people sought the advice of an oracle (see page 17).

The colonists who left Greece moved for good. However, not all of the colonists were welcomed by the people already living in the foreign lands.

This vase painting shows a Greek king directing the weighing and storage of herbs at a colony in North Africa.

12

Magna Graecia

The colonies that were set up along the coast of southern Italy became known as Magna Graecia, or "Greater Greece". The cities of Magna Graecia became important cultural and trading centres.

A temple decoration of the goddess Medusa from Syracuse, one of the biggest colonies in Magna Graecia, founded in about 733 BC.

Greek Colonies

Greek Culture

The people who moved to the new colonies kept Greek traditions and culture alive. They continued to do things the same way they were done back in mainland Greece. As a result, Greek language and culture reached many lands and influenced local art, architecture, farming and religion.

During the Archaic period, the population on mainland Greece increased greatly. In search of new farm land, natural resources and new trading opportunities, people began to migrate and settle in many areas around the Mediterranean and Black seas. These new settlements, called colonies, became important trading centres, and some even became independent city states.

This large bronze vase, found in modern-day France, was made by a craftsman from Sparta.

The Black Sea

The ancient Greeks began to move eastwards, to the area of the Black Sea, as early as 650 BC. Colonies founded in this region provided excellent trading opportunities. The Greeks traded luxury goods, like olive oil, wine, high-quality ceramics and jewels, for wheat to feed their growing population.

Luxury items made by Greek craftsmen have been found in the Black Sea region. This detail comes from a golden comb made in the region.

Sparta

Unlike Athens, which had a democratic government, the city state of Sparta was ruled by a small group headed by a king. The laws in Sparta were very strict. Spartan men were expected to become brave soldiers in service of the state, ready to fight at a moment's notice. Women had the task of raising strong and healthy children. Sport was widely encouraged, even for women, and favoured over the arts and learning.

This vase shows a fierce competition between Spartan wrestlers.

Athens

Athens became a rich and powerful state, the leader of a group of city states who joined together to fight off foreign invasions. Athens grew into a cultural centre during the Classical period. Some of the greatest Greek thinkers, writers, artists and politicians came from the city.

One of Athens' greatest leaders was Pericles. He improved the city's roads, port and agora.

Classical
Greece

During the Classical period the two leading city states, Athens and Sparta, became great rivals. Athens became the world's first democratic state while Sparta became a mighty military power. Many aspects of daily life in these two cities were different. The agora, in the heart of Athens, was a daily meeting place where men shopped and caught up on the latest gossip and political events. In Sparta, sporting events stole the show.

The Agora

This vase painting shows a blacksmith's workshop in the agora.

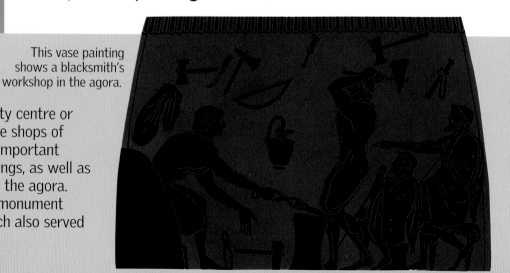

The agora, located at the city centre or near the port, was full of the shops of craftsmen and merchants. Important monuments and state buildings, as well as race tracks, were located in the agora. The agora in Athens had a monument dedicated to its heroes which also served as a public notice-board.

Society

In ancient Greece the family unit was the most important part of society. Households were made up of both family members and slaves. Every member's role was well-defined. Men had active roles in public life, while women were bound to the home, raising children and keeping house. Slaves served and obeyed their masters.

Women were not given any decision-making responsibilities. Fathers, brothers or husbands were in charge.

Bronze statue of a slave boy cleaning a boot. Slaves were people who lost their freedom when their land was conquered by the Greeks.

Democracy

Citizens in Athens had the right to elect their own government leaders and were free to express their own opinions. However, only male Greek landowners were considered citizens. Foreigners, women and slaves had no say in government and were excluded from public life.

Athenian citizens met at assemblies where government matters were discussed. Citizens voted on important decisions, such as the passing of new laws.

Worship at the Temple

Priests and priestesses were in charge of supervising rituals and taking care of the temples.

Religious worship involved prayer and the making of offerings, such as wine, milk or sweets. Altars stood outside each temple so that rituals could be celebrated in the open air where everyone could see and take part. Inside the temple stood a statue of the god or goddess to whom it was dedicated. Greek temples always faced east-west, in alignment with the sun.

The All-Athens Festival was celebrated in June each year. A great procession was held as the people of Athens carried a new woollen robe for the statue of Athena on the acropolis.

Gods and Goddesses

The Greeks worshipped many gods and goddesses. The 12 most important ones were believed to live in a big palace on Mount Olympus. Zeus was the chief god. He was married to the goddess Hera. The other goddesses were Artemis (goddess of the hunt, nature and childbirth), Athena (goddess of war, crafts and of Athens), Aphrodite (goddess of love and beauty), Demeter (goddess of agriculture) and Hestia (goddess of home and family). Besides Zeus, the male gods were Apollo (god of law, music, poetry and dance), Ares (god of war), Poseidon (god of the sea, earthquakes and horses), Hephaestus (god of fire and art) and Hermes (god of trade).

Feast Days

Many feast days and festivals were held during the year. There were farming festivals, days to remember the dead, celebrations for the gods and more. The two main festivals in Athens were the All-Athens Festival and the City Dionysia, when plays were staged and poetry read.

Oracles

The Greeks went to shrines called oracles to ask questions about the future. The answers to the questions were interpreted by priestesses who gave the questioner their reply. The oracle of Apollo at Delphi was one of the most famous shrines.

Religion

This dish shows a man consulting the oracle at Delphi.

Religion was an important part of daily life. The Greeks consulted a god or goddess through an oracle (see top right) before taking any decision, whether deciding who to marry, or whether to go to war or not. Every village and town was dedicated to one or more gods. Athens, for example, was dedicated to the goddess Athena and everyone had to worship her. Greek stories about their origins and gods were preserved as myths.

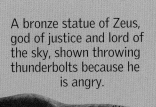

A bronze statue of Zeus, god of justice and lord of the sky, shown throwing thunderbolts because he is angry.

A golden statue of Athena stood inside her temple, the Parthenon (see page 18).

The top of this building is supported by columns in the shape of beautiful women.

The Human Body

The Greek sculptors of the Classical period represented the human body in a realistic way. They studied the relationship between the parts of the body to give each part the right dimensions. They also studied how the body moves and could create sculptures of muscular athletes.

Doric column

Ionic column

Corinthian column

Architecture

The Parthenon is one of the greatest works of Greek architecture. This Athenian temple was built in honour of Athena on the acropolis, the highest point of the city. The architects of the Parthenon designed the building so that each of the architectural elements, such as its columns, were at an equal distance from each other. This created a sense of order and harmony both inside and outside the building. The temple was also decorated with colours and relief sculpture.

This statue of a discus thrower shows the muscles of the body at work.

This is how the Parthenon may have looked when it was built.

Columns

Columns not only supported buildings, but they were also an important decorative element. Greek architects created many designs, like the ones shown above, to embellish the top parts of columns.

Sculpture

Some Greek sculptors created works with a flat background, called reliefs, to decorate the surfaces of temples and other important buildings. Sculptors created figures and fantastic scenes which seemed to emerge from the buildings' surfaces.

This horse's head is a detail of a relief that was made to decorate the Parthenon in Athens.

Painting

Most of the wall and panel paintings that Greek painters created have been destroyed over the centuries. However, fine examples of Greek painting can be found on vases. Painters depicted a variety of subjects, including scenes from everyday life and myths. These scenes tell us a lot about how the ancient Greeks lived.

This black-figure vase painting shows two heroes, Ajax and Achilles, playing a board game.

Art
and Architecture

Art and architecture are perhaps the most studied and admired aspects of Greek culture. Greeks applied new rules to art which were based on a close study of the natural world around them. They created life-like statues, beautifully designed buildings and stunning paintings which brought the stories they depicted to life.

Vase painters from Athens became famous for their skills. Some signed their names on their creations.

Vase Painting

At first vases were decorated with black figures and details were added by cutting into the surface. Then, during the Classical period, new techniques were developed to make the paintings seem more realistic. Artists created red-figure vases. Vase painters drew the scene on the vase and then coloured only the background and details. When the vase was baked, the uncoloured parts turned red.

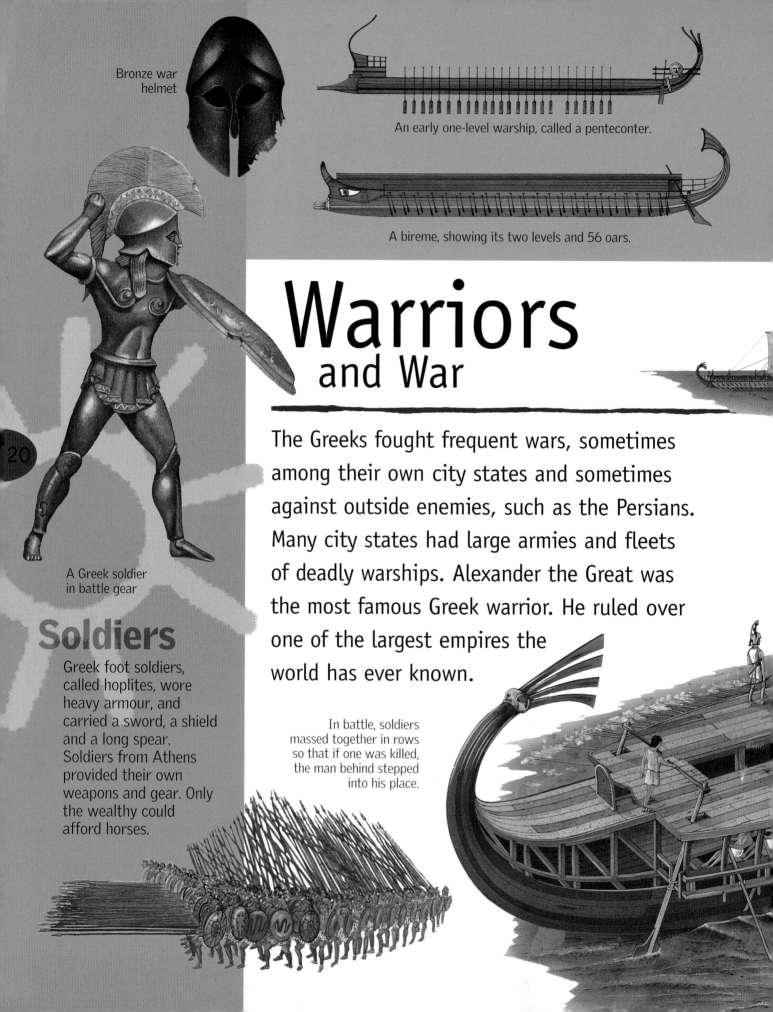

Bronze war helmet

An early one-level warship, called a penteconter.

A bireme, showing its two levels and 56 oars.

A Greek soldier in battle gear

Warriors
and War

The Greeks fought frequent wars, sometimes among their own city states and sometimes against outside enemies, such as the Persians. Many city states had large armies and fleets of deadly warships. Alexander the Great was the most famous Greek warrior. He ruled over one of the largest empires the world has ever known.

Soldiers

Greek foot soldiers, called hoplites, wore heavy armour, and carried a sword, a shield and a long spear. Soldiers from Athens provided their own weapons and gear. Only the wealthy could afford horses.

In battle, soldiers massed together in rows so that if one was killed, the man behind stepped into his place.

Warships

The first Greek warships, called penteconters, had just a few oarsmen on a single level. Then the bireme was invented. This had 56 oarsmen sitting on two levels. Light and fast, this ship was also a favourite with pirates. But it was the trireme, first built at Corinth in about 700 BC, that became the most important fighting ship. With 170 rowers on three levels, it was powerful, well-designed and fast.

This detail of a mosaic shows Alexander the Great riding into battle.

A fleet of triremes being rowed into battle.

Leaders

Alexander the Great was a powerful leader who became emperor in 336 BC, when he was just 20 years old. Within 10 years he created an empire that stretched from Greece to northern India.

Major Wars

The Greek city states were united against their powerful neighbours, the Persians, in a series of wars that raged off and on for much of the 5th century BC. But later, between 431–404 BC, the city states were divided in their loyalty for either Athens or Sparta, in an internal struggle known as the Peloponnesian War.

Plays and Actors

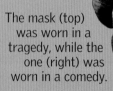

Plays told stories of people and the gods. There were three kinds of plays: plays with sad endings, called tragedies; plays with happy endings, called comedies; and amusing plays in which the chorus consisted of men dressed as satyrs, forest creatures with the ears, legs and horns of a goat. All of the actors were men, even those who played the women's parts. Each actor wore a mask painted with a face to match the part he was playing.

An actor in costume, holding his mask, prepares for a performance.

The mask (top) was worn in a tragedy, while the one (right) was worn in a comedy.

Sport

The ancient Greeks took sport seriously. Sport was not only a big part of young men's education, but it was also linked to religious festivals. At stadiums spectators enjoyed watching athletes compete. Gifted athletes were highly regarded.

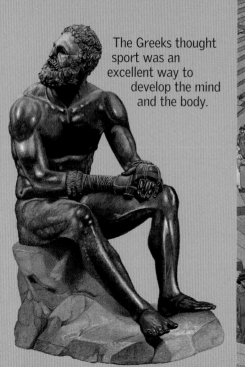

The Greeks thought sport was an excellent way to develop the mind and the body.

The Theatre

Huge theatres were built to hold large crowds. The seats were arranged in a semicircle and faced the orchestra, a circular floor in the centre of the theatre where the chorus performed. The chorus was a group of actors who played music and recited poems during the play. The stage was behind the orchestra and was part of a building used by actors to prepare for the performance.

Music

Music was a big part of everyday life in ancient Greece. Religious feast days, banquets and the theatre all involved music. Music even accompanied the daily routine of labourers and soldiers in training.

A musician teaches two of his pupils how to play the lyre.

This child's toy, of a goose and rider, is made from baked clay. Real geese, ducks and small birds were popular pets.

Theatre
and Entertainment

In their free time the Greeks participated in sport, played music, held banquets and enjoyed plays at the theatre. The earliest performances were part of religious festivals dedicated to the god Dionysus. Since most public functions were only for men, women relaxed at home with their children, enjoying games and lively conversation.

Games

The ancient Greeks played many games of chance. One of the most popular pastimes was the game of knucklebones, which was similar to the modern game of jacks. Players had to throw gamepieces in the air and catch them on the back of their hands. Game pieces were made from sheep or cattle bones.

Knucklebones was a popular game with women.

All men were required to go to the theatre. Poor people who were not able to buy their own tickets were given money so that they, too, could attend.

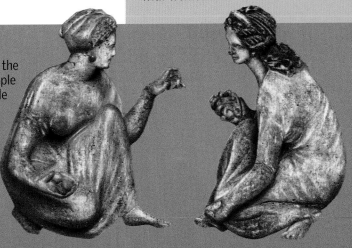

Education

Boys attended school from the age of seven. Students learned to read and write and master the rules of grammar. The major subjects were literature, sport and music. Girls were taught at home. They were trained to become good wives. Few girls learned to read and write or to play musical instruments.

Since schooling had to be paid for, not all families could afford to send their children to school.

Doctors studied plants for their healing abilities. Herbs were used to make medicines.

This carving shows a doctor, attended by a nurse, treating a patient.

24

Knowledge

The ancient Greeks valued a love of knowledge, curiosity and a persistent search for the truth. Greek doctors studied the human body and tried to cure illness. Great thinkers tried to answer questions about human behaviour, judging right from wrong. Scientists, mathematicians, astrologers and engineers pushed learning forwards to greater understanding.

Medicine

Greek doctors became famous for their ability to perform surgery and make medicines. Unlike the doctors before their time, Greek doctors began to study how the body worked in order to find cures, rather than relying on magic.

Inventions

Greek inventors created all sorts of machines and devices to help them carry out more difficult tasks. They invented a tool to keep time, steam-powered engines and pumps. They also invented a machine which used energy from a burning fire to open large temple doors.

Anaximander invented the sundial, a tool used to measure time.

The Greeks used the abacus to make calculations.

Mathematics

The Greeks discovered that mathematical rules could be applied to many aspects of the natural world. They used maths to compose music, calculate and measure distances, study the Earth and the stars, and many other things in the universe. Maths was one of the most important subjects studied at school.

Pythagoras was both a philosopher and a gifted mathematician.

Philosophers loved to share their ideas and debate with others.

Philosophy

The word "philosophy" comes from the Greek word meaning "love of wisdom". The ancient Greek philosophers studied the origins and nature of the world. They asked questions about the nature of people and their behaviour. They tried to find explanations for why things happen and what causes them.

The Greek Diet

A typical meal consisted of bread and fruit, with herbs and honey. Meat was only eaten on special occasions and only the rich could afford it. People who lived near the sea ate fish, but even fish was expensive. Lentil soup was a favourite among the poor.

The wealthy sipped their drinks from fancy cups, many in decorative animal shapes.

This decorative bowl was made to serve fish. Food preparation became an art. Cook books and poems were written about food.

Dinner Parties

Wealthy Greek men participated in dinner parties which were an occasion to eat a good meal and enjoy the company of friends. They ate leaning back on couches and were served by young boys and women, who also provided musical entertainment. Some dinner parties were more formal – men discussed serious topics, such as politics.

Large pots, called kraters, were used to mix wine with water.

Farming

A farmer's life was not an easy one. There was plenty of work to be done all year round. The heavy autumn rainfalls and the hot dry summers often damaged crops. Farmers had to plan carefully when was the right time to plant their seeds.

To prepare the soil for planting, farmers used wooden ploughs, pulled by oxen or mules, to turn over the land.

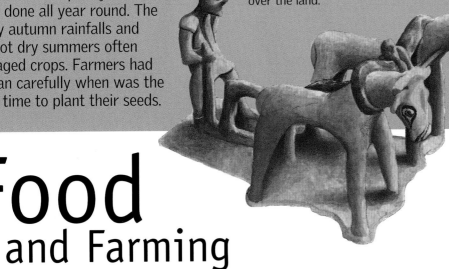

Food
and Farming

Crops

Greek farmers grew many kinds of fruit, vegetables and different kinds of nuts. Farmers were not able to grow large quantities of wheat because of the poor soil condition. Barley, however, was more plentiful. Olives were an important crop. When grain supply was low the Greeks traded olive oil for wheat.

The ancient Greeks made the best of what the land provided. Their food supply came not only from farming, but from fishing, hunting and trade. Although Greek farmers kept many animals, the typical diet for both rich and poor alike did not include much meat. The most important foods were cereals, cheese, vegetables and fish. Almost every home had olive oil and wine on the table.

Large amounts of wheat came from the colonies.

Animals

Sheep and goats were raised by many farmers for their milk and wool. Pigs and chickens were kept too, for meat and eggs. Large animals, such as horses, donkeys and oxen, were put to work, pulling ploughs in the fields. Bees were also kept to make honey, which was mixed with water to make a tasty drink.

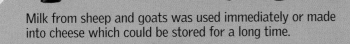
Milk from sheep and goats was used immediately or made into cheese which could be stored for a long time.

Men's Clothing

All clothes, for both men and women, were made of rectangular pieces of cloth wrapped around the body or held together by pins. Men wore long or short tunics which were fastened on both sides or only on one. Over this garment they draped a large piece of woollen cloth. Slaves wore very simple, short tunics which were tied at the waist leaving one shoulder bare.

A citizen, on the left, wears a large piece of woollen cloth draped over a long tunic, while a worker, on the right, wears a shorter tunic.

Greek craftspeople were able to make elaborate jewels, like this gold earring, by pouring melted gold into clay moulds.

Clothing
and Jewellery

Although clothing styles and customs were different from region to region, the ancient Greeks took good care of their bodies. Greek men bathed in public bath houses and those fortunate enough to have a bathtub bathed at home. Clothing and hairstyle told a lot about a person's social status and where they came from. Putting on jewellery, as well as perfume and make-up, were everyday routines for many wealthy people.

Jewellery

Most men did not wear much jewellery. They wore signet rings which were used to seal letters. Wealthy women wore necklaces, ornate earrings, bracelets and crowns. Jewellery was made from a range of materials, from precious metals such as gold, copper, and silver, to materials like baked clay. Children wore good luck charms for protection.

Women used bronze mirrors, like this one, to apply make-up.

Perfume and Make-up

Both men and women used perfume. There were many kinds of scents, made mostly from flowers and spices. Women wore make-up to lighten their faces and make their cheeks and lips pink.

They also wore colourful eyeshadow and darkened their eyebrows. Wealthy women were attended by their slaves who helped them to apply make-up and perfume and do their hair.

The most common shoe was the leather sandal.

Weaving

Women spent a large part of their time making cloth. It was made from wool and cotton. Wool was first dyed and then spun into thread before being woven into cloth. Large frames, called looms, were used to weave thread into large rectangular pieces of cloth which were used to make clothing. Women could make different patterns by weaving threads of varying colours, painting designs and using special materials, such as gold thread.

Women's Clothing

Women wore a large, long rectangular article of clothing that was pinned at the shoulders and tied at the waist. It could have long sleeves or no sleeves at all. The most common fabric was wool while the finest and most expensive clothes were made from linen.

Weaving, an important women's task, was done standing up at the loom.

The most expensive dye was purple, which was made from shells. Insects and minerals were also used to make other colours.

Hairstyles

Hairstyles varied from region to region. In Sparta, children's heads were shaved while in Athens only slaves had shaved heads. Men in Athens had short, simple hairstyles, while their Spartan neighbours wore their hair long. All women, except slaves, had long hair. Women wore their hair up in buns, pony tails or braids, held in place by nets and ribbons. Many women wore hair pieces.

Ribbons were used to tie hair up. Earrings were the favourite jewellery of wealthy women.

The god Hermes, shown here with wings on his feet, was the protector of merchants and travellers.

Traded Goods

The Greeks depended on trade to obtain materials they needed such as metals, food and timber. Goods were transported by sea since the mountainous land made travel difficult. Colonies were excellent bases for merchants and travellers and allowed the Greeks to compete with foreign traders.

This horse-shaped perfume bottle comes from Rhodes. Perfumes were imported from the East.

Trade
and Influence

The Greeks traded crafted goods and farm produce far and wide and the city states grew wealthy. However, the greatest Greek export was their way of life and love of learning and the arts which reached all corners of the known world. Even today, elements of this Greek culture can be found in politics, medicine, sport and much more.

Ports

Ports were a vital part of Greek cities like Athens which depended on trade for a major part of its food supply. The port of Athens, Piraeus, was protected with strong walls which connected it to the city. Many people, especially foreign traders, settled in the port.

Hellenistic Culture

The Classical period was followed by the Hellenistic period. During this time, Alexander the Great ruled over the Greek world. He conquered many lands and spread Greek culture to North Africa and Western Asia. Many non-Greek peoples followed Greek customs and spoke Greek.

A portrait sculpture of Alexander the Great when he was a young boy.

Influence Today

Greek culture is a part of many aspects of modern life. The modern Western alphabet is believed to have come from the Greek alphabet. Also, Greek traditions are still alive today. The Olympic Games bring people together to celebrate the accomplishments of great athletes.

In the late 19th century, the Olympic Games were started up again. Like in ancient times, an Olympic flame is lit in Olympia. The flame is then carried all the way to the site of the games.

Many ideas the Greeks had about science have since been proven correct. The fact that all objects are made up of small particles, called atoms, was originally a Greek idea.

Successful merchants had their own ships and became very wealthy. However they risked losing large cargos to shipwrecks and pirates.

The Greek Example

Not only are the ancient Greeks studied in schools and universities but their ideas about good moral behaviour are still respected today. For example, doctors make a promise, called the Hippocratic oath, named after the Greek doctor Hippocrates. They promise to treat patients to the best of their ability and to share knowledge about medicine with others.

Hippocrates travelled all over the Greek world practising and teaching medicine.

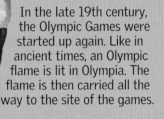

Index